Grow Your Esthetics Income Quickly

Introduction:

This industry is a financial hit or miss. You either hit it, and you are profitable or you miss it, and lose out on potential cash flow. Many things factor whether you are a **financial hit** or **miss,** some things are out of your control and some things are very much in your control. This is a fickle industry, no question about it, and it takes a lot of hard work, resolve and dedication to your trade to be a successful esthetician.

It is sad, but so many schools share success stories and tell future estheticians about the abundance of jobs, but the harsh reality is that most estheticians won't make it in this industry. There are more estheticians than there are jobs, it is just the cold hard facts of this industry—people don't view skin care as a necessity, and if only a luxury, it is the first thing to be cut out of one's budget.

We estheticians could never understand how anyone could cut routine skin care out of their budget, it is as horrible as someone not getting their teeth cleaned—it's just gross, but the reality is we are a select group of individuals. We care about the health and appearance of our skin, we know that taking care of our skin is the difference between a beautiful canvas waiting to be painted, and a cracked canvas that will never quite be as beautiful as it could have been.

We know the health benefits, both emotionally and physiologically of skin care treatments, and we know the power of human touch. The problem is most of America is backwards in their understanding of how imperative it is to take care of one's skin, and overall health. We are a country that feeds on junk food, de-stresses with cigarettes, and indulges in the sun's rays to nourish our overworked and overstressed souls. I wish our society would adopt a more French lifestyle, one of prevention and maintenance equals skin longevity, but unfortunately our society isn't there yet.

If this is true, then why would anyone want to go into esthetics? I don't think anyone goes into esthetics simply for money. Most of us go into it because we love helping other people, we love nourishing the skin and pampering the soul. Of course, we love the amazing tips, and the generous split commissions, and we leave our jobs like we never worked at all (minus the backaches). We get to play with skin care products, make-up, and cool gadgets. We contribute to the beauty of beautiful people, and at the end of the day that feels really good.

This career choice is a delicate balancing act financially. There are strategic things that must be done, must be followed to make good money in this industry. This isn't rocket science, these are simple things that every esthetician should do to generate more profits. It doesn't matter if you are full-time, part-time or only on call—these steps will increase your bottom line, period.

You might not like doing these simple steps I am going to tell you about, but give it a chance, you will increase your profit and be glad you did. This isn't a get rich scheme, this isn't a guarantee-- these are easy steps to incorporate into your practice, a way to increase your cash flow. You ultimately have the choice to follow all or some of these steps, but I hope you consider using most of the steps to increase your earnings and stop leaving money on the table.

You want to make the most money you can while doing what you love, right? You want to work more efficiently, not harder, correct? You want to feel financially rewarded, is that a fair assumption? Then you have to have a plan. You can jump into your esthetics career with absolutely no plan at all; you can take whatever wages you get and live with it; or you can set out to earn the most you can in your time on the clock.

Your employer is not going to do this for you, let's face it, most employers don't care about your bottom line. Their goal is to make the most money for the spa, not you. You want to increase your income stream whether it increases theirs or not, you want to reap the benefits of hard work. **You can't do this without a plan.**

If you are in school now, or you just graduated, I don't want to burst your bubble, but esthetics school is just scratching the surface. I know you are excited to conquer the world at this point, I was too. You can be successful, but you have to work at it, you have to plan, and you have to be confident that you can build a book of business. **Let's face it, nothing that is worth anything comes for free, it is never easy.** If it were easy, everyone would be a success. Everyone would jump on the bandwagon. You have to decide how badly you want this, and how you are going to get there.

I can tell you, I have hit many bumps along the road in this career, but I have always kept my eye on the prize: doing what I love. For me, nothing is more important than earning money for doing what I love. It's that simple. Plenty of people have well-paying jobs, but plenty of people are very unhappy at those jobs. Love what you do, and while loving it, make sure you are earning a good living—what could be better than that combination?

If you are passionate about esthetics, dedicated to learning everything you can about this industry, and are a hard worker then keeping reading this book. If you're not, **my simple steps will never increase your profit.** Only the best of the best survives this industry, it takes high standards in care and sanitation; exceptional customer service; the thirst to always learn; and entrepreneurship abilities, to not only survive, but thrive in this industry. **This is not a get rich book, this is not flipping through some pages to easy earnings; these are real income producing tactics that require work.**

My simple steps are designed to help you increase profits quickly; help you earn more money per hour in less time; and make you a more desirable esthetician. What I am advising are tools that worked for me. I can't promise or guarantee these will absolutely work for you, but it is worth a try. If what you are doing isn't working, if what your spa is doing isn't working, then why not try something new? What do you have to lose?

Let's get you started on making more money, and working more efficiently instead of harder. I know you probably already work hard now, and if you are reading this book, I am guessing you aren't making what you should be. We need to move you from the esthetician who makes peanuts, to the esthetician who makes a good income in a short amount of time, the goal is to provide a good living for yourself while doing what you love.

Remember, you have the power to change your personal situation. Your attitude, efforts, and your professional image will all interplay with these simple steps. This is your chance to move from regular esthetician to great esthetician.

One thing I love about this career is that there are many opportunities, it is a great career for mothers who only want part-time work, but it is also a great industry for people who want to work crazy hours. You literally could work a couple part-time jobs, and you could do vastly different things in this industry to keep it exciting. This isn't your typical 9-6 career, it has so many options and choices that only you can decide if it is right for you.

I've done it all. At the time of this publication, I am only doing skin care product sales, meaning I sell wholesale products to local spas. I have done everything from work for a doctor's office to working for a regular spa to a massage therapy studio, and I have even dabbled with franchises (but I never last—not a fan of franchises). I have also rented my own booth successfully, one of the greatest challenges I ever took on because as a booth renter you are responsible for paying that rent every month along with your advertising and supply costs. In addition, I've operated my own freelance spa party business, which was great fun, but also a lot of work.

What I've found with everything I've done in the esthetics world, is that there is no room in this industry for laziness, no room for excuses, and certainly no room for people who don't dream big! During this time when I ran my own businesses, there were a lot of people telling me to just work for someone else, but I was tired of working for someone else. I had been working for other spas for a long time, and I never had this overwhelming desire to go out on my own, and then one day I decided it was time.

Why did I do it? I got tired of unscrupulous owners, and when I started my first business (spa party business) I did it while I worked at a spa, a nice spa but the owners were cheap and shady. These were the type of owners where I had to double check my paycheck, and the type of owners who would want me to perform Microdermabrasion on clients knowing full well that the machine didn't work. I couldn't do it. So, while I was there, I formed my owned spa party business and then decided to focus mostly on that.

With the spa party business, I was in control of my money. I saw so many spa party businesses pop up, but these businesses were run by people with no industry experience. I decided to open a spa party business backed by the skill and integrity of an esthetician. My parties paid me between $200.00-$450.00 depending on the size and the theme picked. It was a good freelance business that allowed me to be in control of my schedule and income.

   I did it for a while and then life changed in an instant, and my personal life took me in a new direction, in a new place. I had no idea what to do. I knew I didn't want to work for anyone else, but I also knew the area I now called home was not the best area for spa party business, so I decided to take the plunge into booth rental.

I never had a month in booth rental, other than my very first month in operation, that I didn't make money—never had a month that I couldn't pay my rent, supplies, or advertising costs. Some of it was luck I am sure, but a lot of it was strategically thinking and planning on how to make it work in terms of upgrades and retail sales to generate more income.

Then I moved from the treatment room to skin care sales, which is a huge leap because I didn't know a lot about sales. I started part-time while still in the treatment room. I like challenging myself, and it was an opportunity to try my hand at another side of this amazing industry.

I hope this book inspires you to continue doing what you love while educating you on how to make the most money possible. **I am not here to tell you an easy way to success, I am here to tell you easy ways you can increase your profits quickly.** I want you to know the truth about the industry, things that I wish I had known before jumping in without a clue. I want you to know this is a truly wonderful career choice with many opportunities, but I don't want you to think this is an easy career nor do I want you to think the money will just pour in without hard work.

Hard work equals success. I don't know one esthetician that is successful that sat back and let the money rain on them. It doesn't happen. **Successful estheticians have two common ingredients: passion and hard work.** There is no other way to cut it. You can be passionate until the sky glows rainbows, but if you don't put in the work and effort to be successful, that passion won't generate anything of substance.

Here is what has worked for me, both working for someone else and working for myself. These are the top things that generated more income for me while working in the treatment room. Some estheticians are afraid to do these things, but trust me, once you do them a few times, it will become like second nature. Once you get a taste for making more money per service, you will understand the power of these steps. Good luck!

Step 1: Location=Beautiful People=Money

Location rules the real estate market, and you know who else it rules? You got it! The beauty industry. Take a look around, examine where the beautiful people flock, it isn't likely they flock in the run-down areas with vacant land, run down strip malls and weeds blooming like the summer flies. No, the beauties are going to flock to beautiful areas, places with sprouting flowers, gorgeous tree-lined streets, and architecturally gorgeous buildings. Good-looking people are attracted to equally stunning places of business.

I know there is a lot of eye-rolling here, I know some of you are going to tell me you can't help where you live. **You know what that's an excuse, every city has beautiful people**. If you have to drive an hour every day to work to find attractive people, then that is what you have to do to add money to your pocket. I never said this would be easy, this isn't the easiest route. This is the most lucrative way to add revenue to your esthetics' income.

Estheticians complain, and they complain some more about money. They can't earn enough money, or the shop they work at doesn't have enough business. In most cases, it takes me only five minutes to determine why they are failing: location.

It is probably one of the single, most important decisions you will ever make in your career, determining your location. You need to work in a wealthy area, with lovely people who will invest in their looks. It doesn't matter if you are renting a space, or you work for someone else, you must be in a top-notch location.

The reality is you are looking to increase your revenue stream-- the easiest and fastest way to do that is by only doing business in expensive places that draw in the beauty conscious crowd and doing so in a high traffic area.

You might think that is discriminatory, and that you won't limit yourself to pricey zip codes, but if you don't make location a top priority then you don't want to make great money. This is a beauty driven culture, and money drives beauty. Beautiful women pay to maintain their beauty, if you think all those striking women you see on the streets are born that way, think again.

You have what these women want, you have power to help them improve on that beauty with your esthetics' license. They want your services, and they will pay a premium, but every day women won't. I know some of you won't like this, you will say all women deserve esthetics services, and that is true but ask yourself if you want to be the esthetician making marginal money with the everyday women, or if you want to be the premium esthetician who makes more money.

You might not like what I am saying, and I am sorry about that but we are here to make money, not hand out charity services. Would you work for $15.00 an hour if you could work for $40.00 an hour for doing exactly the same job, but in a different location? I think many of you would scream up and down the spa halls at the thought of increasing your hourly by $25.00 an hour. It is true, you can increase your hourly significantly depending on the location. I know this is true because I have worked in cheaper places, and extremely expensive places, and I vowed I would only work in upscale areas because I can make so much more money in less time. It is basic economics, it is working more efficiently and increasing your earning potential in a fraction of time.

Let me give you a real example of how I know this to be 100% true. I worked in a very pricey zip code where basic facial were between $75.00-125.00. Then I worked in a place that unfortunately the zip code didn't lend itself to commanding high prices, and the average basic facial was around $30.00-50.00. The tip on these services, for the one starting at $75.00 was at least $15.00-$25.00 for 20% and above tipping scale, and yes all these customers tipped 20% and above on a regular basis. So, if I did the cheapest facial at $75.00 and I got the cheapest tip of $15.00 (which was rare) I made $37.50 (I had a 50/50 split) plus the $15.00-dollar tip put me at $52.50 without any retail sales. If I sold the low end of my retail products, let's just say $40.00-- I had a 10% commission structure on all retail (that I negotiated up front) so I just added $4.00 to my $52.50 an hour bringing my **grand total for the hour to $56.50**. Remember, this was **the lowest I could generate at the wealthier location**. Imagine what I did with the more expensive services.

Now, at the other location where prices started out a lot lower, my earning potential plummeted, thus I vow to never work at a location that doesn't command high prices, it just doesn't make sense to my bottom line. So, let's say we did the very basic hour long facial at $30.00 and the tip was 20% at $6.00. That is a total of $36.00 for the hour. That is a huge difference. At most of these lower end spas, I find it is hard to negotiate top dollar for retail commission, so let's just say that they still gave me 10% (unlikely at a place like this, but it keeps it easy) so on $40.00 of product sales that would be $4.00 still. If I was on the same 50/50 split (which I wasn't—again found these types of spas more at 30-40% max) but for argument's sake, let's just say I was at 50/50 to keep it similar to my wealthier location, I would be at $18.00 for the facial, $6.00 for the tip, and $4.00 for the retail sale for a **total of $28.00 per hour.**

If you compare the two scenarios, that is **a $28.50 difference.** That is huge! Do you want to work harder for less money, or do you want to work the same degree of hardness for a lot more money? If I did just 4 basic facials at the lower end spa with all the same tips and retail sales, I would have made **$112.00 that day**, but if I did 4 basic facials at the higher end spa I would have made **$226.00. That is double the money! This is the power of location.**

I don't know about you, but I love this career, but I still want to make more money. I put a great deal of effort into my work, I always give a top-notch service whether the person is paying $30.00 or $100.00 for a facial, so why shouldn't I be compensated grandly? The choice is yours, and only you can decide how you want to work, but for me it makes better financial sense to double my income with something as simple as the location.

Quick tip: In my own experience, I've learned that the higher end locations not only generate more money, but the clients are less fickle. They listen to skin care advice and retail suggestions, and they are willing to not only tip handsomely but they are also willing to spend money on retail. Most of the clients in less affluent areas, tend to tip less than 20% and rarely buy the retail products, some of course do, but I would say the majority are not buying into the need to purchase retail products. At the affluent spas, those clients want to know everything about good skin care, and they are willing to buy it, no matter the cost. Just something to think about.

Now, let's talk a little more about increasing that hourly even more. More? Yes, absolutely. Push that hourly up more. There are several ways, and I will expand on those in the other steps, but for now I want to focus on **TIPS.** This increases your income exponentially, and while there are many things you can do to help improve tips, and I will share some ideas about this later in the book, it is important to think about prices of services. In the menu of services, the treatment prices dictate what type of tip you will be able to command. Of course, some people tip less or more, but on average if you expect to get 15-20% standard tip, the higher the service price the better the tip rate. Again, in the affluent areas, expect 20-30%.

If you're a new esthetician, your instructor might not have explained how this all works, but it is important to think about this in financial terms to your own wallet. It is easier to get a larger, more significant tip at an upscale establishment simply because the service prices are higher. How easy is that? What an easy way to increase your paycheck?

Please do not underestimate the power of working for an expensive spa. It can contribute greatly to your bread and butter. It is the proliferation of your revenue cycle.

My goal isn't to steer you away from the middle income areas, my objective, and what I think yours should be if you want to make more money, is to consider location as a serious contender in multiplying your profits. I assume if you are reading this book, you want or need to generate serious income.

It is simple supply and demand. This beautiful client base needs estheticians, where the lower income areas might look at it as a luxury. If you fill a need, you are providing a service that is an absolute necessity and people will come back regularly. If it isn't a need, people will only come when they can afford it. In the last scenario, your paycheck might shrink in comparison to the upscale scene. I would rather drive further to work, knowing I can command top dollar than stay in my own area that might not command as much money.

Ultimately, it is your decision, but the goal here is to increase your profits. You are here reading these pages to learn how to evolve into a financially successful esthetician, not one who is barely making any money. A treatment at an upscale spa and one at a low-end spa can make the difference between making a substantial income, and mediocre one. It comes down to the old saying "Work smarter, not harder (author unknown)." I don't know about you, but I would rather work smarter and for more money than working harder for less money. It's just plain, financial commonsense.

This doesn't mean that you shouldn't work for less money. If you found a dream spa with a wonderful owner, but they charge less for treatments, then it might be a consideration despite the financial losses. Always think about how your choices in employment, in terms of the location, will affect your income.

Quick Tip: Negotiate the best shifts. Stalk your spa! Go visit the spa that you intend on working at on various days and times, and see when it is busiest. Those are the days you want. You don't want Monday morning

at 10AM if they have zero customers. **Negotiating the best shift puts more money in your pocket, why sit around making no money, if you can be booked on the busy days?**

Step 2: Skip the Franchises

Here we go again, I'm going to ruffle some feathers. I apologize for upsetting any of you who might be offended, but I am here to tell you ways to increase your profitability not tell you what you want to hear. Do you know why estheticians don't want to hear **"skip the franchises?"**

A lot of estheticians love franchises because simply put they hire almost any esthetician, with or without experience. I think it is great that these places give new estheticians an opportunity to work there, so don't get me wrong, **if you are just starting out and need work experience by all means try them out.** If you go down this road, with most franchises you won't be able to negotiate your salary or commissions, but if this is where you land, you can work on giving the best service possible to increase tips and rock that retail so you can try to earn extra money per hour. This isn't my preference for any esthetician, but it is a good place to gain valuable experience. However, I don't think you can control your own financial destiny as well as working for a private spa, or for yourself at a franchise.

This is all about increasing your salary, and my focus is on that, but if you are new I don't want you to think that I am hating on franchises because that isn't true. I think they serve a purpose, but they don't make my list in terms of increasing your income. However, they are a great place to get your feet wet and build a resume. I don't find that most estheticians make a great deal of money at these places, and they are rigid and structured. It doesn't mean they aren't right for you, and it doesn't mean there aren't some estheticians that do make money there, but my experience with them (and with many esthetician friends) is that they have high turnover for a reason. I think their structured system forces estheticians to hit a financial glass ceiling.

Why avoid franchises? In my opinion, most of the facial/waxing franchises that I know of offer low-cost facial/waxing services, and they generally pay by the hour. What is wrong with hourly? Nothing is wrong with hourly per se, but commission splits generally pay more. In addition, the cost of the service is lower than upscale spas which brings down your tip income potential. You are being paid a lower per hour rate, usually not much more than minimum wage and the owner is the one reaping the financial benefits. In addition, you will work hard, very hard—as they seem to want to get every ounce of hard work out of you!

Some of these franchises will tell you how to earn more money by upselling. That is absolutely true, but not really with franchises. The owner retains most of the money when you upsell at a franchise, you don't get much of a cut, and that is true with retail sales. The only person earning significant money on these up sales and retail products is the owner. They will tell you how much you will make by doing A, B or C but in truth you don't make as much as they do. It truly is unfair in my opinion.

I can't find any reason to work for a franchise unless you are new and need experience, or you are an esthetician that likes the security of an hourly, and you don't feel that you can venture off into the world of commissions. That's okay, that is a personal decision, but I am here to help you make more money, and if that is what you want too then avoid the franchises. Now with that said, if you are skeptical about going out on your own, the beauty of this industry is that you could work part-time at a franchise and have the security while building up your own business on the side.

Don't wealthy people frequent franchise spas? I am sure some do, but most wealthy people have more discriminating tastes. They want the newest and greatest treatments, the finest skin care lines, and they like a non-cookie cutter environment.

There are probably good tippers at the franchises too, but again with the quick in and out service and the cheaper prices, the tips are going to scale down in comparison to the upscale spas. The bottom line is---are the majority good tippers? There will always be outliners at any place, at the upscale spa you will have cheap tippers occasionally too, and at a franchise spa you will have an occasional extravagant tipper, but what you are looking for in terms of increasing your hourly rate is the median rate at these places. **Where is your most potential to make the most money in less time?**

If you are reading this as a new esthetician, it might be valuable to try to get two esthetician jobs, one at an upscale spa and one at a franchise for the purpose of comparing the income stream. It certainly would be an interesting research project, but more importantly it would help you determine the difference in income levels.

Quick Tip: If you plan on making money via the franchise method, make sure you know at the time of accepting the position, what the commission structures are exactly. A lot of times, the managers are fast-talking and gloss over the exact methods to achieve the higher commissions. Make sure you have all this information in writing, and know exactly what you need to do to get on the path to making more money at the franchise.

The other negative drawback to your hourly rate at a franchise is that there isn't much loyalty building. It is tough to build a regular client base. You can build a decent client base, but not in the same way as a boutique spa that offers a more personalized service. At the boutique spas, you have the opportunity to connect with your clients more, offer them a little more pampering where the franchise you really need to focus on providing a fast-food turn around type of service. On the plus side, the franchises spend a great deal of money advertising so they bring in a lot of foot traffic.

The lack of a loyal following equals less tips and sales, which in turn equates to a lower income for you. It might not seem like a big deal, but every little bit helps increase your hourly rate, and when you make decisions as to where you will work, you want to think about how all these little intricacies affect your bottom line.

When I say this, I am speaking from my own experience as I have dabbled with franchises early on in my career, and I have followed many careers of my fellow estheticians that have worked at franchise wax places and massage/facials stores. We all agree that it is a fantastic place to get your feet wet as an esthetician, and the consistent money is appealing to some, but in terms of growing your income these types of places might not be at the top of the financial scale.

Step 3: Freebies

I love freebies. Who doesn't? And one thing I love doing for my friendliest customers is giving them freebies. **Think about it for a second, you can increase customer loyalty and happiness by simply giving them something for free!**

Of course, this depends on your budget, and if you work for yourself or an employer. If you work for yourself it is pretty easy, you control your freebies a 100%. It can be as simple is giving them a free collagen mask, a paraffin hand dip, eye brow or lip wax, or anything else you want to give away. Really these things are fairly cheap—almost free. How much does a little bit of lip wax cost? What about a paraffin hand dip? These things are easy to incorporate into a treatment for a fairly low cost, but it helps connect you with the customer. They think you are doing something special for them, and that helps build a loyal following. Why would they go to someone else when they can go to you and get extras?

What if you work for an employer? This is a little tricky, and you have to be careful on your approach. I also gave away freebies while working for someone else. I never gave away anything of substance, but I might give them a little collagen eye cream, or a free scrub. I made sure to tell the client that they were getting an upgrade, but I kept it quiet at check-out. Why did I do this? Simple, it was an easy way to have the customers rebook with me. They would come back because they knew that I would always take care of them—that means more money in the long run. It also means bigger tips now. Most of these customers would offer larger tips because they knew they got the best service, plus some!

When I worked independently, I would give away free treatments based on what services weren't selling well—partly to introduce those services (so they would book them in the future) and to make the customer feel like they got something extra.

For example, I had an organic peel that just wasn't popular, not many people were booking this service. I decided to give this away for free to my best customers, I made sure that I talked it up so they would tell their friends about this organic peel, but I gave it to them as a free add-on. What happened? Most of them loved the peel and returned for future peels (more money) and they tipped me more money because they got something for free.

What does giving away free services have to do with earning more money? It makes customers feel special, it makes them feel like you went above and beyond for them, and it creates loyalty to you. Why would they go to another esthetician who only gives them a basic service, when you give them an outstanding service with freebies?

I don't know about you, but if I get the rock star treatment for the same price as the basic treatment, I'm going back to the person who pulls out the red carpet for me. That is just common sense. I want the most bang for my buck, and I am going to tip accordingly.

When I gave away these free organic peels, sure I lost money in my product that never took off on the service menu, but what I gained financially was so much more than the cost of that one bottle of organic peel. My tips were explosive when I gave away these services, and my rate of re-bookings were rock solid, and my referrals were extraordinary. All of which equal more money.

It is something so simple, so easy and yet many estheticians refuse to give away anything for free in the fear that they will lose money. And at first glance, it does appear that you are losing money, but you have to look at your rate of return. ROI, return of investment, and yes, this an investment—talk to your tax adviser about what freebies you can write off. You are investing in increasing profits through a greater tip base, return customers, and word of mouth. Many of my new clients came from these clients that I took care of because word gets around when you give the best service combined with freebies.

I had moms recommending me to their daughters. I had chess club ladies recommending me to their friends in the club. I had women who played golf recommend me to their golf friends. The list went on. The power and money that comes in from treating your clients well, and from making them feel like they are getting something for free is quite extraordinary marketing.

What if you work for an employer? How do you get away with giving freebies without getting fired? This is a little tougher, but I've been there, and I understand the delicate balance of this particular situation. You need to go with your gut on this one, and I am not advocating you do anything that might get you fired.

I worked for this spa that was all about the almighty dollar, and giving away anything for free, even time was the crime of the century. I had some fantastic customers that deserved special treatment; they deserved the red-carpet treatment; they deserved the above and beyond pampering experience and yet I was in a rock and hard place because I couldn't offer them anything without going against company protocol.

I had to get creative, and I had to think about how I could keep them coming in for services. How I could get them to continue to book with me, and to give generous tips? I decided I had to do something that didn't use more company product, something that didn't take too much extra time, and something that would increase my revenue stream simply by making the customer feel like they won the facial lottery.

I invested in spa rocks, they were mine not the spa's rocks and I would offer hot and cold stones as a free option to add to facials. I would use cool stones for the face, warm stones for the chest, shoulders, head, and to the feet (check your state laws).

For my peel clients, I would offer a warm lotion treatment for their hands and feet, I had to invest in booties and gloves, but I can't tell you how many clients adored these simple treatments. It cost them nothing extra, and for me I only had to invest in the lotion, booties and gloves (available at spa stores). Before we even started the chemical peel, my clients were already relaxed and on their way to happiness.

Another client favorite, and this one is so simple, was a heated, cushion eye mask that I sprinkled with a relaxing scent, and I would put it on them during a mask. My clients were in love, it added to their relaxation and again it created a sense of satisfaction, it was more than they might get from another esthetician and it was free. The other estheticians working at this spa weren't doing these extras, they were following the company's standard facial protocols, and essentially giving money away.

The key to offering free services is to balance it, you don't want to give everything away for free. My rule of thumb is to offer every new client something special, make them feel like they are your only client and take care of your good clients.

The goal is to keep the clients coming back, getting referrals (and don't be shy about asking for referrals) and offering such a stellar service that the client has no choice but to leave an amazing tip. If you are working for an employer, you want to take a careful approach as to how to handle this situation, but the ideas above allowed me to add freebies and huge benefits to my customers without stealing anything from my employer. This is very important! Anything you give away for free in terms of products should be owned by you. If you want to add a peel or collagen mask, make sure you buy your own from the same supplier, and keep it in your tool kit. The last thing you want is your employer to fire you, or worse call the police and say you were stealing products. I would recommend labeling everything that is yours with your name to avoid any confusion.

Customers like to feel like they are unique, and that you treat them better than the next customer. Who doesn't want to feel special? Who doesn't want to feel like royalty for a moment in time? Isn't this why they come in for pampering? They want to be taken away from the normal stress of life; whisked away into a relaxing and calm environment with an esthetician that takes extra care of them. This is going to be a place that they want to frequent. If they frequent your spa, it puts more money into your pocket.

Plain and simple, it is old fashion customer service. In this busy world, with the standardization of facial spas, we lose the exclusive spa environment where no two services are identical, even if they picked it off of a menu. What brings in more money, is creating a treatment that disengages the cookie-cutter generation that we all have recently been indoctrinated with and moves towards distinctive new class of treatments from an era gone by.

It wasn't too long ago that facial treatments were only for the wealthiest women, even upper-class women couldn't always afford the star service that used to be synonymous with estheticians. It was an upper crust society that could rub elbows with estheticians, it was an extremely expensive endeavor to have regular treatments.

I think that is what is missing from much of today's esthetic services, it is that classical approach to esthetics. It is this new fast-food for facials; the quick turn-around; the cheaper skin care products; and the lack of customer service that is driving this industry down.

There will always be customers that flock to coupon spas, even facial franchises for their deep discounted membership prices, but the women who will ultimately pay the higher price tags, are those that are looking for something exclusive, something of higher quality.

It doesn't mean that there shouldn't be affordable spas, and there is a place for it in the industry obviously, but it isn't the piece of pie that is going to put more money in your pocket. The people winning the financial rewards in this scenario are the owners, and the franchise corporations. The estheticians should be getting a larger piece of the prize here, the estheticians that are creating the loyalty and following, and the estheticians who work a laborious job to build a book of business. These franchises reap the benefits while the estheticians get little reward. Sure, you might be thinking a steady paycheck is a heck of a reward, it might be to some, but to me it is keeping estheticians from making bigger money. Again, this is all about personal choices; I prefer to work more efficiently and reap the most financial rewards for my efforts.

You have to decide what type of service you want to offer, and what that means to your bottom line. For me, I knew that I wanted to be in the upscale establishments, not just for money but to be around that exclusivity that would allow me to create a unique environment. I don't want to provide assembly line esthetics, I want to provide a unique service and treat each customer the way I expect to be treated. While I use service menus, even when working for myself, it is the fact that no two services are exactly alike for me that I love. I can change them according to my client's needs or change it on the whim because I am not stuck in a cookie cutter environment. That is hugely appealing to me, and I like to get my creative juices flowing. I like to be in control of not only my time in the treatment room, but also the potential earnings.

Before I went into esthetics, I had a long hobby of getting all kinds of skin care treatments. I loved skin care products since my early teens, and by the time I was eighteen I was getting facials. I had facials everywhere from traditional spas, to hair salons, to doctor's offices (this was before the launching of what we now know as Med-Spa) to cruise ships. I worked to get treatments, and while I couldn't afford to go every week, I saved so I could go at least every other month. I thought nothing of spending $75.00 on a facial, even back then, because I knew the benefits of receiving regular facials were worth every penny. I learned at an early age, that most women who had beautiful skin in their later years, were women who took care of their skin and sought the advice of an esthetician.

These experiences make me the esthetician I am today, in fact, I didn't realize how many students go to esthetics school and have never had a facial before! What my years of getting these services taught me was the difference between a good service and an outstanding service. It demonstrated why one esthetician commanded a high-priced service (and a large tip) and why others really only deserved a coupon, discounted type of rate.

There is a distinct difference in levels of customer service, passion, and the level of pampering that goes on in these spas. I am happy to report, most of my experiences were fabulous, but there were times that I had a few horrible experiences where I felt like the esthetician slopped on some product and didn't care about their touch, there were times the esthetician left me for fifteen minutes while a mask was drying instead of increasing the level of pampering with a scalp or hand massage. I only returned to the best estheticians, and I worked hard to take what I learned from them and establishing the same high-quality treatments in my own room. These were the estheticians that could command top dollar.

When you think of freebies, now keep in mind how those freebies translate to the customer. How does it make them feel? You might not see the value in freebies, but I assure it might make the difference between a large tip and a mediocre tip; it might mean the difference in no referrals and several referrals; and it might equate into many more re-bookings. It is definitely something to consider, and it is really easy and fairly inexpensive to incorporate.

Do you have to go the extra mile and give freebies? Absolutely not, you don't have to do anything, but I highly recommend taking care of those who write your paycheck. In addition to service freebies, it is a welcome gift for a client to receive a few token skin care samples. This does two things: makes them feel like they got something for free (again you taking care of them) and it allows them to sample the product line if they are on the fence about purchasing.

With all my new clients, I offered a tiny fortune cookie box from a craft store filled with one skin care sample and a business card. The fortune cookie box was very cute, I found black and white paisley boxes, and I wrapped them with a light green ribbon. Most of the customers were enamored with the box, and excited to see what was inside. I like that it is a gift, it makes the first experience even better, but it also introduces them to the product line and it gives them information (business card/with hours).

Quick Tip: Shop the dollar aisles of craft stores. In order to fund my adorable freebie skin care samples and business cards, I purchased only dollar items. The fortune cookie boxes were 4 for a dollar. The ribbon was a dollar for a roll of it. Get creative. It doesn't have to cost a lot of money to create an exquisite looking gift that speaks to your clients.

Depending on where you work, you might be limited in giving away freebies, in that case, I would recommend you purchase sample sizes out-of-pocket and distribute them to clients, so you can get them to purchase products from you. Another option is buying sample size bottles and putting a portion of the product you are using on the client for a treatment and send them home with a tiny bit to try. Jell-O-shot containers are a great way to do this (instead of containers), and then you would need a marker to label the container.

I haven't worked for one spa that was on board with giving out free product. I get it, it's costly to buy these products, even sample sizes at wholesale. It is a cost of doing business, but that doesn't mean you should give every person a sample, be prudent. Like I said, I only gave new customers this gift, but throughout the year I would give my other clients freebies in either service or product. Sometimes it might be a mini-sunscreen; sponges; a lip balm; or in most cases a free service.

Quick Tip: Always ask your boss about giving away samples first, put the financial burden on them prior to you spending any money on the samples. Or ask them to consider opening a skin care bar area, a fun place to sample everything.

I wish more owners would realize that while product is expensive that many clients don't want to spend money on a product without trying it first, especially those clients who are used to drugstore prices. Yes, we all know that drugstore quality products lack the effective ingredients for skin to radiate, but the customers believe in the mega marketing campaigns, and don't understand the value of the high-priced products unless they can sample it and see the difference.

A fun alternative to the above is to ask your employer if they would open a skin bar where you could have a sampler station for clients to try before they buy. It is also a way to open up dialogue about their skin care concerns beyond the treatment room and gives the client an opportunity to look at their skin in the mirror. It is a great place to hang around when you have no clients, be available when clients from other therapists (massage therapists, hair, nails, etc.) are leaving and invite them for a free skin analysis. Another great one is makeup, you could also have a free makeup demo. You will be surprised at the number of people you can book by engaging them with this fun, conversational piece-- the skin bar station.

In my experience, freebies are another marketing tool to promote products. When I was in practice, I never had to hard sell anyone, in fact, I didn't have to sell anyone at all. I simply educated them, gave them a sample, and let them decide if they wanted to buy. In many cases, the gesture of giving them a free sample alone got them to buy future products. **My paycheck growing at a rapid rate was due to product sales and upgrades during treatment, I could avoid selling altogether, or I could increase my rate of pay exponentially.** One thing I would like to make clear though, I never sell a client anything I don't believe will truly benefit their skin, and I never sell anything that I think is junk, period. My integrity is more important than money.

This is another area where I take issue with franchises, the estheticians are trained to sell, sell, and sell— even if the client already has that product. The goal is to always sell no matter what, and I am a firm believer that in doing so, the relationship with the client is destroyed. The client no longer trusts the esthetician. Yes, you make a lot of money in retail, but don't sell them something they don't need just to make a buck. There is a fine line here in managing your integrity and making more money, keep it honest.

Step 4: Adding additional licensures

Esthetics is one of those fields where it never hurts to have additional licensures in related fields. I am telling you this from experience, countless dollars that I gave away because I wasn't a massage therapist. Seriously, I can't tell you how many customers requested me to do their massages but by law I wasn't authorized to do those massages. Now, let's put this in perspective, the massages at the place I worked at were anywhere from seventy to hundred dollars, and my split was 50/50.

I don't know about you, but to me, that was a lot of money I gave away. In addition, the tip on those services would have added more fat cash to my pocket. I let it slip right through my hands and passed it off to one of my massage therapist friends. I was completely against going to massage therapy school, but think about it for a second, it is absolutely genius to have both licenses because you cross-sell yourself, and if your book isn't full you can book your facial client for a massage right after the facial service ends.

Not only does it increase your book of business, but it adds serious cash to your bottom line, simply by having the additional licensure. It is great way to acquire more business, expand your client base and add to your cash flow. My massage therapist friends were constantly busy, and if I could have gone back and done it over, I would have unequivocally gotten a dual license.

The opportunities there are truly endless, but having any additional licensures is extremely helpful. The receptionist/staff can promote your list of services at the time of booking, and the more you can offer, the more options you have. Now, with that said I don't think anyone should necessarily be a jack of all trades because there comes a point in time where you need to find a market niche and know what you are good at. **There is nothing worse than being able to do everything yet being good at nothing.**

When I worked at a med-spa they had a unique client base because they were affiliated with a foot doctor who saw patients for diabetes. What's so special about that? These patients needed special care when they received manicures or pedicures due to the delicate nature of their diabetes; cutting in the wrong place could mean serious health consequences for these patients.

This was another great lost opportunity for more cash in my pocket. It was one more thing I couldn't do, sure I could do esthetics, but it is easier to build your esthetics clientele if you can talk up your services to your other clients. With nail customers that is easy, they talk to their nail technician while they get manicures and pedicures, and it is just one more person who knows about your services. A nail license would have served me well at this particular spa, and certainly would have increased my income.

The thing about med-spas that makes them unique today compared to when they first cropped up is that they are more of all-purpose shops than traditional medical spas. Honestly, so many med-spas really aren't real medical establishments, the only way they get away with calling themselves a medical spa is by having a ghost doctor on staff, meaning the doctor is only on the books to collect a piece of the pie.

I don't know that I like the new wave of med-spas, but what I do know about them is that the more services you can offer, the more you can cross-sell yourself, and the more in demand you will be. You will make money due to all the services and higher tips, and you will likely be able to renegotiate your commission spilt and ask for a higher rate. If you can do multiple things, if you are the go-to therapist then I would ask for a 60/40 split, meaning you get

60% of all services. The owner can baulk, but it comes down to what added value you offer the spa. This is true for any industry, the more valuable you are the more money you are going to make.

The spa world is truly your oyster here, and esthetics may be your only true love but don't discount all the additional ways to add money to your salary. It doesn't mean you are walking away from esthetics at all, it means that esthetics is one part of your business now. That was my mistake, I frowned upon doing anything else because my first love is simply esthetics. I didn't want to become a massage therapist or do nails, and that was a bad decision on my part.

Another fantastic license to add to any esthetician's resume is an L.P.N. which is a license practical nurse. This is your fastest route into working for a cosmetic surgeon or dermatologist, and not only does it add credibility to your esthetics license it can add a lot of additional money to your income. There is no doubt about it, it is much easier to get your resume noticed at a doctor's office with the L.P.N. at the end of your name, it is just one more licensure that will catapult your career if that is the direction you want to go.

Check your state laws, but some L.P.N's can do cosmetic fillers, and assist with surgeries in a cosmetic surgery practice. In addition, they can work with dermatologists doing more invasive peels and assisting with skin cancer removal. If I wasn't scared of needles and blood, this would have definitely been an option for me because I think the whole practice of dermatology is absolutely fascinating, and cosmetic surgery changes lives---what a great industry to be in.

The nursing degree bumps up your potential earnings, it means you are more powerful contender in the job market, and it adds expertise to your resume. I wish this was something I could do, but a nurse who passes out from blood and needles would probably get me fired on the first day.

If you like science, and if you don't mind needles and blood then by all means consider this licensure as another top rated one to add to your esthetics license. Health care is one of the fastest growing industries; look through any employment site and you will see the demand for nurses. Couple a nursing degree with esthetics, and you have the potential for a very interesting and lucrative career.

On the topic of needles, if you don't mind poking people with needles, acupuncture is on the rise. It not only commands a lot of money per session, but people are flocking to it for health and stress reasons. This might seem very different than esthetics, and it is to a degree, but esthetics is about health too and anyone compassionate enough to be an esthetician certainly can be an acupuncturist.

Depending on the spa you work in, I am thinking organic here and less medical spa, you can build up a nice multi-business practice by doing esthetics and acupuncture, and again you can cross sell. You have to like science for this one but having had acupuncture myself I can tell you the tranquil environment is very much like the spa environment we estheticians are accustomed to. It is another cash cow, and finally the western part of the world is experimenting with the medicinal qualities of it.

What I love about acupuncture is that it doesn't fit into traditional medicine, but it has healing properties. Many estheticians don't think about the healing properties of the human touch in esthetics, but we are healers in a non-traditional aspect, and with acupuncture it is another level of healing. Who thought those little needles could actually feel good? I know I just said I hate needles a few paragraphs above, but I love the acupuncture needles. For some reason they soothe the soul, they bring you into balance and peace. With the additional earnings you could make, I highly recommend this an option to add to your career repertoire.

For the creative soul, another great license to add to your esthetics license is a cosmetology certificate, if you are person who loves color, fashion and the latest styles then this might be a great one to add to keep the money flowing. This is one of those professions where you will have a lot of time to talk to the clients, and plenty of time to cross sell your esthetic services. How easy is it for a client getting a haircut to add a mini-facial to their appointment? Why would they see another esthetician when they already have a connection with you?

Quick Tip: Dual enroll in esthetics school with another license as the same time. It saves you time, and possibly money if you could do both at the same time.

I wish more esthetic schools would encourage students to pursue multiple licenses, even do "what if" scenarios with esthetician students and demonstrate how significant it is to have a backup plan in esthetics. **There**

will be days in esthetics when you will be swamped, but no one talks about the days when the appointment book is as quiet as a cemetery. I know this sounds harsh, I know it might not be what you want to hear, but it is the reality of this industry. I would love to say this career is bustling with opportunities, but the truth is beyond hard work, there is a lot of luck involved in being a successful esthetician. Go through the want ads, and you will see that there aren't a ton of jobs for estheticians. That doesn't mean you can't get a job, it just means it is harder than some other industries.

Forgive me if I am the bearer of bad news, I am not trying to burst your bubble. I love the esthetics bubble too, but I want you to know the reality. Esthetics is a fantastic field, it really is the best career, especially for mothers and people who only need part-time work. In other words, it is easier if you have another source of income from your spouse, another job, or you're independently wealthy. Yes, there are some estheticians who do make it big, and they never have to worry about how to pay the bills because they hit it big, and yay for them, but my goal here is to assume you are like the average esthetician and you need a real way to make money. **You need a nuts and bolts approach to succeeding in this job market.**

This is why considering adding an additional licensure is so important, it can be the difference between an excellent paycheck and horrible one. As you learned above, there are so many intricate details that contribute to higher earning potential with additional licensure, and the more customers you can cross sell the more likely you will earn more commission, sell more retail and upgrades, and gross higher tips.

It is basic economics, you are making yourself more valuable which in turn makes you more money. I know you might be huffing and puffing right now, there is probably some eye-rolling too, I know you don't want to go back for more schooling. I get it, none of us do, but unfortunately to stay on top of our game in this industry we really need to make ourselves invaluable in the industry.

You want to be the busy employee at your spa, right? I assume you wouldn't be reading this book if you didn't want to be the best, if you didn't want to earn the most money and have a following. You are here because you want to work more efficiently, make more money in less time and create a career, not just a job. That's what I want for you too. I want you to learn from my early mistakes, and my biggest mistake was not getting a secondary licensure to compliment my esthetics license, and to expand my profits, period. Unequivocally, this is my biggest regret.

Now, with that said please don't go accumulate a ton of student loans because I said to consider a secondary licensure. My point is to simply put it on your list to think about, ponder and analyze if the amount of money you have to spend to get the licensure will add up to enough increased revenue over your work life to be a reasonable venture.

We all have to come to terms with the high price of higher education, and we ultimately decide if it is worth it or not. Unfortunately, any kind of training is expensive and we all need to weigh the benefits against the risk of having that student loan hanging over our heads.

In consideration of a school for any secondary license, be mindful of the prices. A lot of times the admission rep will present all the bells and whistles and make the hefty price tag seem worth it because you can borrow the money today and pay later. Remember, you still have to pay that money back, and you have to be careful and make sure your earning potential is much greater than what you have to pay back.

For a secondary licensure to be worth it in the long haul of your career, you should try to figure out how much money you think you can add to your revenue stream per year with this license, and how much you have to pay for the student loan in a year. There are several calculators on the Internet that will calculate your student loan payments.

I am not a financial advisor, so please be cautious when taking on more debt. Learn about the schools and how the prices compare to other schools so that you can make the best financial decision. Remember, my goal is to help you increase your salary not put you so far in debt you can't afford to eat every month. I want a secondary license to increase your income stream, not hurt you. So please weigh all your options out carefully.

I've presented a lot of different licensure choices here, but that doesn't mean you should register for every school and be a jack of all trades. I think sometimes being a jack of all trades is worse than only having an esthetics license because you never get good at anything. Eventually your income will drop because you aren't any good; you aren't an expert at anything and your quality of services reflect that.

I would recommend trying to find your niche area, and only add licensures that make sense to that area. If you want to work in a day spa, adding a massage or nail license would fit in well. If you decide to go the med-spa route, an L.P.N. license would add a lot of credibility to your resume. If you want to go in a more organic route acupuncture would be helpful, and if you decide that the beauty world, and all its colorful glory is your thing then by all means add a cosmetology license to your resume.

No matter what you choose to do from the list above, these different licenses will only help you soar to new career heights, and the money will follow. Also, do if from the heart, if you pick something you hate because you think it will make you money, I am sure disappoint will come. Do something that you will enjoy, and that combination with esthetics will generate much happiness and money.

Step 5: Product Sales

I know most estheticians hate sales! I get it, it can be uncomfortable asking someone to buy something that they don't think they need. In addition, professional skin care products are expensive, no way around it. The better the product, the more expensive it usually is, and the customers are going to challenge you as to why they should pay more money for this product instead of going to the local drug store and buying it for peanuts.

Product sales is one of the fastest ways to increase your income stream, but you have to do it smartly. First of all, you want to negotiate a better rate of commission on retail sales with your employer. This is easier to do when you work as an independent rep instead of a franchise where you are an employee. I always ask for a standard 10% at the start, but sometimes you will have to settle in between there. You can also ask if they do any bonus plans or offer perks or incentives for you to sell more. Some offer a horrible rate of 2-3%--it is more money than selling nothing, but if employers want you to sell and promote products they need to reward you with decent percentages—only you can decide what that number is. I would implore you to negotiate your product sale percentages at the time of your hiring (in writing).

Secondly, you need to sell products that customers can't easily buy online, if they can buy it online it gives them time to shop prices and that means zero commission to you because they will ultimately find it cheaper online. Just a quick side note here, I always remind my clients that when they buy their skin care products from our spa they can guarantee it is fresh, and it hasn't sat around in a warehouse for a year. A lot of times, these reduced priced skin care products are from spas that went out of business, and a company buys the products at auction, and during that time the products sit in a warehouse and blow by the expiration date. Cheap customers won't care, but clients who care about efficacy of those products, and its usefulness to their skin will absolutely take pause and listen to you.

Selling products is all about delivery, it is an art. You have to delicately balance educating the clients about why they need the products, and how the product will improve the skin. It is important that you believe this to be true, otherwise you are just lying. It is also equally important that the skin care product does what you say it does, or you lose credibility.

A lot of estheticians fear product sales, and for good reason because the customer might decline and they feel it puts them in an awkward position. We tend to think of sales as a seedy, unethical and a money driven group of people, and we don't want to associate with that. I am the first one to agree with that, I would never recommend that you sell products that your clients don't need because that is when you cross the line between being honest and the seedy sales person that will sell anything and everything for a quick buck. Don't cheapen yourself to that level. You will find some franchise places will push you to sell everything and anything, and I would use caution in these scenarios.

Quick Tip: Make sure you have a return policy. I guaranteed if my clients didn't like my skin care products after purchase, they could return it within 5 days of purchase. I knew that my products were great, and that a return was highly unlikely. It makes people more comfortable about purchasing, especially if you don't have a sample of the particular product you are selling. If you work for an employer, ask them what their return policy is on products.

Fortunately, for us estheticians our clients do need our products. Many clients use over-the-counter junk that is exacerbating skin care issues and ruining their chances of achieving a blissful glow. How this turns a profit for us is educating the customers on how the products can make a difference in their lives, and why they need it. You have to show them why the over-the-counter product isn't going to change their skin and create a need.

The thing is, over-the-counter products, even doctor recommended, isn't likely to change the skin the way many professional products do, and it isn't going to give the customer a beautiful complexion. Most the over-the-counter, doctor recommended brands, are recommended because they have no irritating scents, not because they are game changers for the skin. They don't drastically make a difference in the appearance of the skin.

These very customers wouldn't put generic food in their bodies (okay some might) if they could afford healthier versions of the same food, right? The customers have to equate the product with health, you almost have to paint a picture of the fillers and chemicals in over-the-counter products, so they can get a true understanding of how those products take away from skin health, rather than facilitate healthy, beautiful skin. Some will still balk and buy the drug store junk, but many will conform and slowly make the change, and you will see the changing results as they visit you each month. I've seen the difference myself, clients who fell for the marketing propaganda of these drug store deals, and their skin looked horrible until they got on a professional regimen.

I always tell my customers that if they have just $25.00 dollars to spend, then spend it on a high-quality cleanser that is specific to their skin needs. I explain that this $25.00 bottle will last for a while, if they are conservative and use a pea-sized amount. Then I go further and tell them to slowly start getting rid of the over-the-counter product lines, and every month try to incorporate a new professional skin care line to their regimen until they have all the pieces they need. It slowly introduces them to the products, and feeling and seeing it converts them. This also allows them to psychologically make the financial investment, once they see the value they will want to buy the products.

In addition, I always give out samples. Beware! Some customers play the-give-out-samples game, and they will try to get by on samples to save money. When I had new customers, I always gave them two samples of our product line specific to their needs. Yes, it cost me some money, but it gets customers hooked on the products. It is a try-it-before you buy it way of getting them to convert. (Check with your tax adviser about deducting this as a marketing expense).

I do not try to convert clients simply to make money. If I have clients who are using a high-quality product line at home, I encourage them to wait and buy from me when they run out of that line. Sure, I lose some money now, but there is a balance between making money and doing what is right. I won't sell anyone anything I don't believe in 100%.

Here is an example of that, I worked at place that sold weight loss body wraps, and the whole retail product line to go with these wraps. The owner would embellish greatly on how much weight a person would lose with these so-called weight loss body wraps. She would measure their inches before and after the wrap, and she would tell them what a success the wrap was because they lost a lot of inches.

It crushed my soul to watch these poor women, these desperate women who wanted an instant weight loss miracle, to believe they lost weight when they looked no different from when they walked in the door to when they left. It was so shady, and I think these weight loss wraps should be banned. The loss of inches came from the compression wrap, the person was wrapped for an hour in a tight compression wrap that squeezed their skin together, no wonder they lost a few inches after the wrap process.

I am sure I would have been fired on the spot for this, but anytime a client asked me if they would truly lose weight with these body wraps, I would tell them the truth. I told them that I could not recommend it, and to me it was far smarter to exercise and eat right. "Spend your money on good health, not a body wrap that promises inches lost, of course you will lose inches because of compression. As soon as the compression releases, you are going to be exactly the same size you were when you arrived."

I can't tell you how many clients thanked me for being honest. The owner probably couldn't understand why the body wraps weren't a hit, but I couldn't sell them something that I knew was a huge stretch of the truth. I don't feel bad about the loss of business, sure I lost commission off of it, and I lost the tips associated with it, but at the end of the day feeling honorable is more important. You are probably wondering why a book about increasing your profits would turn away business, but you really have to decide if your integrity and good reputation is worth doing something you believe is wrong, and I believe the weight loss wraps were a deceitful way to make money.

Some of you probably sell weight loss wraps, and I am not here to judge your particular weight loss wrap, it might work for you, I don't know. I am talking about the wraps we did with a sports bandage and a heating chemical, in my opinion, it did not grant the results the customers thought they were paying for. I could not and would not promote them because I knew they didn't work.

When you sell, make sure you can live with yourself at the end of the day because it is your reflection that stares back at you that is important, not your boss or anyone else. There is a balance between increasing our profits, and I recommend doing what you can to increase your profits but do it with integrity.

Selling, educating, and earning money from doing what you love is a beautiful thing. The best part about retail sales, aside from helping your customers achieve beautiful skin is that you significantly increase your hourly rate. You can work in extra money for doing virtually nothing—just recommending a product.

I examined my paychecks closely and realized that the trend in selling both retail and upgrades exponentially increased my rate of pay per hour. Let's say I made $35.00 for that hour just for commission, no tip on that one, and then I did the same facial the next hour, but I sold product. Now, if I had a 5% retail split on a $40.00 product which is a whopping $2.00—seems like chomp change, but that took me to $37.00 for that same facial. If I sold multiple products I could be up over $40.00 per hour. If I did that every day with every customer I would increase my income by $10.00 a shift if I only did five facials in a day, or $50.00 in a week, without adding in the tip amount.

Then when you get to a point where you can negotiate a higher commission split as I did at my last job, I got 10% of the retail sales so that same $40.00 product paid me $4.00 which took my $35.00 ,50% split to $39.00.

These little details make a difference because they all add up. When you sell two products instead of one, it makes a big financial difference in your hourly. Every time you sell something you are adding more money in your pocket, and **when you add upgrades to retail sales you are starting to see higher and higher return on your hourly rate.**

So how do you sell without coming off as pushy? That is tough because everyone's personality is so different, but I try to educate people. I never push. I ask them what they are using on their skin in a non-confrontational manner and ask them what changes they would like to see in their skin. I explain how the products will change their skin, and why what they are using can't do the job (if it is a bad product). I am extremely cautious in my approach, and I watch body language and personality to make sure I am not offending the client.

In most cases, my products sell themselves when I do the service. The clients will ask me what I am using, and they tell me it feels good or smells divine. Then I take that opportunity to talk it up a little bit, but not in a sales' aggressive way. Towards the end of the service, I tell them that I am leaving a few products that I highly recommend helping improve their skin with the receptionist. I always tell them there is no obligation, and it is up at the front desk waiting for them if they want to take a look. I never stand over top of them and make them feel pressured into buying. It has to be their choice.

Selling in esthetics is more about teaching the customers the difference between drug store and professional products. They think if it is labeled in green writing and claims to be organic then it must be. They have no idea what they are putting on their faces, and how it affects the appearance of their skin. While they think they are saving money, in the long run they are spending more money because they are going to need more treatments to fix their problematic skin, due to poor skin care product choices.

It's a tight rope between educating and not offending them, it is finding that tipping point that will make them understand why they need these products to have the type of skin they want. Is it easy? No, not always, but eventually you will learn to build a rapport with each person that walks into your treatment room, and it will get easier every time.

There are very few people a day who walked in my treatment room who didn't have products waiting for them at the front desk. I had a dermatologist client that I never sold a darn thing to for obvious reasons. She simply came to me for relaxation, and she knew far more than I knew about skin care and products that she didn't need my advice, and she could write herself scripts for the best products on the market. So she is one of the ones who got away without purchasing any products, but it isn't often an esthetician has a client who is a skin care expert on the treatment table, and just so happens can write their own scripts and administer their own Botox. Most of your customers will need your advice.

Have you seen some people's skin lately? Look around at people and observe their skin. Yes, people need the advice of estheticians, even some of the so-called experts at the beauty counter could use a good esthetician!

Never feel guilty about selling skin care products, you are doing customers a favor by helping them attain more attractive skin. There is nothing wrong with helping them do that while earning extra money for yourself. My opinion on this one is simple, as long as you can live with yourself at the end of the day, as long as you feel good about what you're selling then there is no reason to feel bad about it. In fact, many customers want to do know what you recommend, so if you don't ask them, they might just go to the nearest drug store and ask the cashier for her advice, and we know that would be bad. Many customers think the women at the local drugstore and makeup counters are experts. The companies call these women "beauty advisors" so the client trusts them.

Learn to love sales, learn to educate people, and always maintain confidence. If you let customers see that you are scared, (and the first time you try to sell something it will be a little scary) they will smell the fear and question whether the product is really useful for them. Always maintain poise and self-assurance because the minute you lose that, you've lost that customer. You won't be believable, and no matter how great that product is, they won't trust you enough to buy it.

Sales is a great way to make a couple extra dollars per hour in the treatment room. Is it going to make you rich? No, but it sure does help coupled with all the other steps we are talking about. Remember, every little bit moves you closer to your financial goals. Besides, why would you work more hours, when you can make the same amount in a shorter time with these simple tools?

Step 6: Upgrades

You know how I said to learn to love selling retail? I am going to say it again about upgrades? If you are new to the field, you might not know what upgrades are exactly. It is anything that you can upsell to the treatment scheduled. If you are doing a standard facial, and you add a mini-peel or Microdermabrasion, that's considered an upgrade. Adding an anti-aging hand treatment, a Vitamin C Mask to the neck, a deep scalp and hot oil massage, reflexology, hot stones, a makeup application, tweezing of the brows, a back facial, and anything else you can think of, or that your employer will allow, is an upgrade. Some upgrades are suited more for booth renters, or people in private practice because generally your employer determines the daily specials of upgrades. However, if you work for an employer I would highly recommend asking them to offer upgrades, so you can add to your profit level. Some owners don't think about the cash cow of upgrades, and how that adds a lot to the bottom line. Particularly, if your employer is a big Internet coupon junkie, I am sure you know the two heavy hitters in the industry that drive down our spa commissions, if your employer subjects you to these coupons than adding upgrades will help tremendously.

Quick Tip: At the start of every service, I placed a laminated "Treatment Add-on's-Today Only" menu with my add-on services and prices of the day. Every customer got one on the treatment bed, and before I started the service, I asked them if they wanted to upgrade today. The laminated add-on sheet is a great way to get them thinking about what a deal the add-ons are…I like to use a lot of color with these as well. I generally used one for a two-week period, in case customers come back they don't see the same repeat add-on's over and over again. I've done everything from coconut-lime back facials, to hot stones, to glycolic peels, to anti-aging hand facials, etc.

What I love about upgrade sales is that they are so easy, and profitable. I worked at one place where the owner had the vision to offer a daily promotional special, every day it would be something new. One day it would be a peel for $20.00 with any facial, the next day it would be a $10.00 Microdermabrasion with any facial, and on another day it might have been a collagen mask for $15.00. The point is, every day there was an option to upgrade.

The thing about selling is that you will get many "no's" but if you don't ask you can't get to the many "yes's." I can tell you from personal experience that upgrades are a big bulk of the business, if you can sell upgrades you increase your ability to make money.

Here is a scenario to digest, I have a client coming in for a mini-facial at $30.00. At my 50/50 split that is only $15.00, and many of you are probably only working on a 40 percent split so it is even less money. Now, if I sell our daily special which let's just say it is a $20.00 peel, and the owner gets $10.00 and I get $10.00 added to my $15.00. I am at $25.00 without my tip. Assuming the customer leaves 20% which I find most leave that or more, then that is a $5.00 tip bring my total earnings to $30.00 for a half hour service.

You might be wondering how adding an upgrade wouldn't increase the treatment time…in some cases it does, but I always tried to sell upgrades that were easily added to the regular treatment, thus not changing the treatment time. The upgrades for me, became a large portion of my hourly rate, they were like getting bonuses every week for doing something fairly passive. I didn't do a lot of work selling the upgrades and adding the upgrade usually didn't require a lot of extra time. It was a simple step that increased my hourly rate. I always asked every single person, at the time of booking, and again at the time of service (even if they said "no" at booking) if they wanted to take advantage of the day's upgrade special.

You don't want to run late for the next appointment, but you don't want to cheapen the service either, so you have to be careful about how you give the upgrades, and what upgrades you give. In some cases, it isn't up to you, your boss will determine the available upgrade and you have to make it work.

I find that when I work for other people, I have to adapt and organize myself so that I fit into their model. Like or not, when we work for other people we have less control on business operations, and if we want to keep the job we have to fit their mold. I worked at one place where they literally gave me five minutes to turn a room over, it was horrible because I wanted to take my time to really deep clean and prepare the room for the next guest. I had to learn to adjust and find a way to turn a room over at a rapid rate of speed to keep my job.

What I love about upgrades is that they can be fun and profitable, especially if you are in private practice. If you are in private practice, or if you are in school and intend to go into business for yourself the upgrades can get as creative as you like. You are in control, you get to decide what upgrades to offer and the prices—additionally, if you are business for yourself you don't have to split the upgrade commission, it is all yours.

Upgrades are just an additional piece of the money pie, and it is something you should consider. In fact, I think it is more lucrative than retail sales depending on the commission split and cost of the retail item. Interestingly enough too, customers like to hear about upgrades, and a lot of them think they are getting a deal by getting that upgrade of the day. It is a win-win situation for everyone involved, the customer gets an additional treatment at a fraction of the menu price, the owner earns more money, and you earn more per hour with a very simple industry trick.

Step 7: Rebooking

If this is the first time you have heard about rebooking your client, then you missed a big portion of your esthetics education. One of the first things every new esthetician learns is to rebook their clients. This simple step is often overlooked, ignored, and quite frankly is giving money away.

Hopefully, you work for a spa that understands and values the rebooking process and trains all reception staff to rebook as well. Rebooking guarantees that you will continue a steady flow of earnings, and it will build your book of business. It also keeps the clients on a set schedule, if they don't have an appointment time, they might languish between their current appointment and the next one, meaning money lost.

Often spa owners will expect clients to rebook but offer them no incentives to do so. Estheticians and other therapists will wonder why clients aren't rebooking. Is it that they are too busy? Maybe they don't know their schedule, or maybe they don't like to commit right there on the spot. In either case, it is potentially lost business.

I know some of you are thinking that you can't force a client to rebook, and that is certainly true. Many clients won't want to rebook at the time of service. You never want to push them because if you do I can promise you they won't return. Spas are a dime a dozen, and yes you may think you are the best esthetician in the world, but I guarantee no matter how good you are, if you push hard to rebook you won't retain the client.

Spa owners, and estheticians in private practice need to think about incentives. Everyone likes incentives. You go to any retail store anywhere today, and they offer a loyalty card of some sort. Pretzel stores offer every 6th purchase you get the 7th pretzel free, cable companies offer $25.00 off for referrals (speaking of referrals—always ask your clients for referrals), and the list goes on. So how do you offer an incentive for rebooking? Simple. Offer something for free.

There is no right or wrong way to do this, and you can get as creative as you want to figure what incentives attract clients to rebook. I like to give them a free mini-treatment with their booked treatment, meaning they don' get the free treatment today (because we all know they would likely cancel just to receive the free gift), but when they return for their next appointment that was previously booked, they will be rewarded with a free treatment or gift.

You can make the gift mysterious, and they won't know what the free gift is until the day of their appointment, or it can be something simple as a percentage or dollar amount off of each rebooking. It could also be a small retail product. Anything goes, but it is about getting the clients to come back, and who doesn't like something for free?

Rebooking is not the easiest aspect of esthetics, it depends on your practice, but I personally think selling retail and upgrades is far easier than rebooking any day. People want to come back, but sometimes they need an incentive to come back, and those incentives help to keep a steady cash flow for you.

You need to have some type of incentive program for them to want to rebook. Each spa does it differently, but you can offer anything from a free brow wax with their next service, or you can offer a product—you can offer anything that creates incentive to rebook.

What about when a client books, but changes their appointment? I personally would still give them the gift if it was close to the same appointment time from the original time, but some spas have a rule that the free gift is only for rebooking's that are kept. That is up to you and your boss to decide, or if you are in private practice you get the right to figure that one out.

Quick Tip: I like Style Seat's online booking system (most accounts are free) **if you fail to rebook, the system sends them a reminder to come in for a visit.**

The one thing we know is that rebooking's are an integral part of keeping your business healthy and lucrative. In this industry, we don't want spa hoppers, we want to develop and nurture loyal clients who will come to us for years to come. What do you do to motivate your clients to rebook? Simply rebooking the majority of your clients will increase your cash flow because there will be less time between each booking, and that is more money in your pocket.

Step 8: Newsletters

In this modern world, everyone is so busy that they don't stop and take time for themselves. They forget, they put themselves behind the long to due list that they have each day. How do you attract clients to come back? You can offer the mega deep Internet social media coupons, but I am not a fan. I think that attracts spa hoppers who are only looking for their next cheap service, I don't use them and I never buy them. Personally, I think those type of coupons leaves upscale clients questioning a business's quality standards and has them wondering if a business does dirt cheap coupons than maybe they are desperate for business for one reason or another. That's me, I know some people who love these coupons, but I do not use them, and I will not work for an employer who uses them.

What I do like is bi-weekly newsletters. I had more and more clients tell me that they love reading the newsletters that come in their weekly box with skin care and health tips along with favorable loyalty coupons. Many times the clients would tell me that they simply forgot to take care of themselves until they got our newsletter and saw we were offering a promotion.

In most cases, a newsletter will include some type of discount, but not like the crazy coupons I mentioned above who take 50% of your profit. These newsletters discounts will allow the esthetician to still make money while enticing customers. The newsletters are a lot of fun to create, design, and promote.

At one spa I worked at, I volunteered to write a bi-weekly piece. Just a short blurb about some interesting skin care fact, new science, or must have product. Short and sweet is the goal. People don't have time for a long, winded newsletter. Our newsletters would introduce hot product lines, new therapists, and the latest menu services. In that newsletter, the client would find a special coupon that could only be used on a certain day, or with a certain package.

It surprised me how much attention these newsletters garnered, and the rate of return we got on a simple e-mail newsletter. It cost nothing but time to put it together. Truthfully, it was fun to create inspiring, professional, and lucrative enticers.

Anyone can do this, you don't have to be an expert writer or super creative person. I promise you, if you just get started, and try to put something together, your personal style will shine through, and customers will want to pay you a visit.

What if your employer doesn't want to do a newsletter? Bummer, not sure why any employer wouldn't want to reach clients, but I would bring it up in your next meeting and offer to manage the newsletters. First of all, for any future spa employment it will look good on your resume to have marketing and newsletter writing experience. A lot of spas are looking for people who can market and help in that department. Secondly, whether your employer can see the value or not of sending out a professional newsletter, it is good for your business to reach customers more frequently.

Think about this for a second. If you work in a place does massage therapy or cosmetology, or even a doctor's office—you have a whole plethora of potential clients who may not know about your esthetics' side of the business. That is a huge cash cow waiting to be tapped into, and you aren't going to go after it. If you aren't willing to go after it, I would question your entrepreneurial spirit because that is wasted profit, period.

In addition, your regular esthetics clients need to see what is going on at the spa. They need to know what new services you are offering, or what specials you have going on. The Internet along with texting offers a whole new arena for reaching our customer base and bringing customers back into our spa.

The same goes for social media, you definitely want people to LIKE your page and you want to be active on that page. Again, if your employer isn't working the social media angle, I suggest you offer to run that side of the business and get people in the door. It will increase your income so consider the time an investment in attracting more business for yourself.

With social media you can get crazy creative, you can do all kinds of fun posts to attract clients. Are you sitting around on a rainy day praying someone will call for an appointment? Instead of hoping for a client who wants a service on a rainy day-- post a picture of a woman dancing in the rain and offer a rainy-day special for anyone who calls and makes an appointment for *the rainy day special*! You will be surprised how a colorful picture along with a special will get people in the door.

Sports fans? Think of fun days where you can offer a funky, make- up service to coordinate with a sports team. I don't know what your home town teams are, but let's say you are from Baltimore, you could have a ladies "Purple Power" make-up day. Think about how fun this could be. Women want to get all dolled up before a game day, or a game party—how fun would it be to go purplicious crazy with glitter and makeup?

Earth Day? How about offering a flirty, fun, and organic specialty treatment on that day only for a rock bottom price? Add a cute picture of something Earthy, and you have a fun attention getter on your social media page.

Quick Tip: Constant Contact creates beautiful newsletters. It tells you how many people viewed the newsletters.

The thing about newsletters and social media pages is that you are in charge of creating something spectacular that drives business back to your spa, it is up to you to get the creative juices flowing and money coming in.

Don't think of this as a chore, think of it as a fun way to earn more money. Something simple and so inexpensive can bring in more dollars. Remember to change it up all the time, don't let the customers get used to the same thing or they will get bored, and never run so many specials that they won't book normal appointments, if your specials are run too often they will wait for the deal instead of booking a normal treatment.

Keep it fun, energized, and watch your profits increase.

Step 9: Negotiating a Favorable Commission Split

If you are in private practice, or intend on going into private practice very soon, this section won't make much difference to you. However, if you are like the majority of estheticians, you will likely work for an employer either as an employee or an independent contractor.

Read, read, and read some more of your contract with your employer before signing. You need to know every detail. You might just be thrilled to have gotten a job, and right now you don't care about commissions or percentages but trust me the day will come that you wish you negotiated for yourself.

Right now, franchises seem to pay between $8.00-$10.00 an hour and 5% commission on retail. Usually there is no wiggle room in negotiations with this fast-growing franchise spas, and as I said earlier I am not a fan of them. I don't like their fast-food turnout of clients, lack of quality, and their drive to push estheticians to sell anything and everything with little financial reward for the esthetician.

They have a purpose for some estheticians though, they offer new estheticians experience, and I don't want to steer you away if you need that. These are great places to get some experience if you are fresh out of school, or if you just want to get paid hourly and aren't concerned with making a bigger commission split. That is okay too, no judgement on my part. Each is to their own. It isn't a personal choice for me, and I don't generally recommend them, but that doesn't mean my opinion is the only one.

Now, for those of you who want to work in an independently owned spa, this is where we get down to business. You have every right to negotiate with these people, and quite frankly if you don't you are throwing away money. You are in charge of your career, run it like a business.

There will be some owners that will laugh in your face, and they won't give you anything over 40/60 split, meaning you get 40% of services and they get 60% but that doesn't mean you shouldn't try. Again, this is a personal choice, but I always try to get more than 40%. Some expert estheticians can get upwards of 60% but that is rarer than the standard 40%.

Quick Tip: Tip Minimums: Caution about this scenario. Some employers will advertise they pay an hourly rate, which they will do but they use tip minimums to fund the hourly rate. They use a formula where they take a percentage of your tips to guarantee an hourly rate for you, it depends on each agreement, but you might not receive more than hourly until you make a certain percentage above how the employer pays you. Read all documents concerning this agreement.

I personally feel like my time and experience demand at least 50%, and I ask for it. In addition, I don't want the standard 2-5% on retail sales, I want 10% and I ask for it. Some say yes, and some say no. The beauty of our industry is that we can take the lower percentage and wait until we find a spa that will give us the percentage we want. This is a transient industry, it isn't uncommon for people to work a few months at one place and move on. I am not advocating job hopping, instead I am advocating for the best financial situation for you. This is even more important in this industry, we seem to have our share of unscrupulous spa owners.

At the end of the day, this is your career and your income. While we like to think that our employers will take care of us; reward us when we do a good job; and agree to favorable terms-- that just isn't the case very often. We have to be own advocates, and that means negotiating and reading every document before we sign any contracts.

Commission splits seems unimportant to many estheticians I speak with, they are more concerned with getting a job, any job. While getting a job should be the top of your to do list, if you want to make the most income in the least amount of time, you have to consider strategic negotiations as part of any employment package.

Many people outside of the U.S. learn about the art and power of negotiation early on in life, they never pay full price. Life is a negotiation for them. However, here in the U.S. we have this mindset that we have to put our tail between our legs and accept any offer, the first offer without even so much as asking for something more.

Why? Are we afraid of confrontation? Probably. Are we afraid that the answer might be "no?" Absolutely. We don't like hearing the word *no.* Does it make us seem greedy? Possibly.

We shouldn't be afraid of confrontation, this is our career and our income, employers need to realize estheticians and other therapists are their bread and butter---treat us well, or your bread and butter is leaving.

We are all secretly afraid of being told "no" but really the worst-case scenario is they object to your desire to get a higher percentage, and if you don't get it, then you can either choose to work under their terms or find another place of employment. Don't let the fear of rejection scare you, this is business and you have to go after what you want. Money isn't going to pour out of the sky— your employer isn't going to give you a higher split on your first-year anniversary—you have to ask for it when you have the most power, at the time of hire.

Sure, some employers will baulk at you requesting a higher commission split or percentage, but it doesn't make you greedy at all. It demonstrates your business savviness, and your power of negotiating what is mutually fair and agreeable terms to both you and the owner.

Please don't confuse asking for what you want, with going in the spa with a diva attitude and demanding the world. I am talking about maintaining your professionalism at all times, and simply starting a conversation about what works for you both employment wise. It is about taking back some of the power respectfully and doing so with integrity. If you are fresh out of school, you might want to hold off on this type of negotiating until you have more experience under your belt.

This is true for any job, you don't have to accept the first job offer that comes along without asking for a bump in salary. The time when you will have the most power is when the employer wants to hire you. If you ask for more money, additional percentages or commissions after you start working there, it is highly unlikely that the employer will concede. You've lost your power to negotiate at this point.

If you want to increase your income, you have to believe you are worth the higher percentages and commissions. For me, I confident that I can sell off the shelves, and upgrades are extremely easy sales for me. I know in advance that I am an added value to any spa just based on my previous sales, and I can go in and ask for more money. If they only pay me 2-3% I am not going out of my way to try to sell, especially when I know what their markup is on wholesale products. Who is winning on this deal?

Think about this way. On a $40.00 bottle of sunblock at retail, the spa who only pays 5% in retail sales to you- retains $18.00 of this $40.00 sunblock and you get $2.00. Come on, it is a huge win for the spa. If you bump up your retail sales to a 10% percentage you earned $4.00, they still walk away with $14.00 for doing nothing but let you sell it.

I don't think a lot of estheticians think about how little they are being paid for retail, and how much the spas earn. I quit one of my jobs, I wasn't a fan of one of the owners and left, and a month later the other owner called me and asked me to come work for her at a new location. Why did she want me back? Why was she willing to give me the pick of my days and hours? Why was she willing to increase my rates?

Simple, because she knew I could make her easy money with retail and upgrade sales. I don't mean to come off overly confident, but my goal is to make you see the power in your abilities, and what they are worth to spas. This owner was willing to offer me a job at a new location, after quitting the other location simply because I could sell—yes, that's what she told me. She told me I out sold the other team of estheticians in retail and upgrades. That was a powerful statement. Spa owners want estheticians that can sell because it means more profit to the spa, and that means more room for negotiations for you.

Sometimes as estheticians, we are so meek and accommodating that we forget to ask for what we deserve. I am guilty of this as well. I think we estheticians in general are so used to nurturing and pampering others that we ignore our needs, and what is best for us.

The next time you get offered a job, really look at the details of the offer and make sure you are being paid fairly. Remember, you are the bread and butter of the operation, and there is nothing wrong with asking to share a little piece of the money pie, especially if you know you can sell. There is power in being a retail beast.

Step 10: Gift Coupons

I loved giving out beautifully created gift coupons because they helped fill my empty appointment times and generated more money. What exactly is a gift coupon? It is a free service. I only offered it to current clients, and it was for referrals. Basically, I created a beautiful coupon that said "A Gift for You" and it stated that the person could receive a free basic facial. My current clients were gifted the coupon, and then they could give it to a friend. In the coupon, it stated that they could upgrade to the full priced facial for an additional fee—usually between $25.00-35.00 depending on what services I was giving away. I sometimes would offer an aromatherapy facial or a peel combo that could be upgraded. The coupon had no cash value, and it had to be used in a specified amount of time, and it was for first time customers only. At the time of booking, I asked the future client if they wanted to upgrade to the full service for an additional fee.

I only gave them to current clients because I didn't want a lot of people coming in off the street, in other words I wanted to know where the person came from. I didn't give these coupons to bad customers, I gave these to the best customers. Why? I wanted more clients like them to return. I didn't want to attract junk clients, I wanted to attract high quality clients so I gave them to current high quality clients.

This is such an easy thing to incorporate into your business. I created a beautiful "A Gift for You" on high quality paper. Every good client received one of these coupons to give to their friends or family, and all the future clients booked the upgrades, and I increased my revenue stream when I otherwise wouldn't have had that money coming in.

Quick Tip: Use color—or hire a company like Vista Print to do the printing for you. You want these special coupons to appeal to the visual senses so your current customers will actually give these out as gifts.

When I did this at first, I was a little shy about giving them away. I was afraid my customers would be offended that I gave them a coupon for a free mini-facial FOR SOMEONE ELSE, but I was wrong. Many of those high-quality clients gave them to friends, and all those friends upgraded to the special I was offering that month on the coupon.

It was a great way to obtain new clients, and at the same time I generated more income while getting creative and trying new coupons to see what worked. It was fun creating new ideas of what I wanted to promote that month. For me, I would look at what services weren't being booked as often, and then I would offer that as the upgrade for the special price.

Offering something for free can be a dangerous game, you might wind up with a lot of people who just come in for the freebie. That is a possibility, but I found that if I was cautious and only gave these coupons out to the high-quality clients, that I got a huge return in value from this.

It makes people feel like they are getting a deal, and in reality, they still were getting essentially half off the service menu pricing by taking advantage of this deal. It is an opportunity to make money on down times, and in most cases I only offered this coupon during those times that I knew wouldn't fill as fast as another time. The power comes in that you have a new client: new tips, new commission, and new rebooked clients=more money in the future.

A lot of estheticians will rain on the parade here, they will say this is bad business because you have to offer up a free coupon to get them in the door. Yes, you do. Yes, by doing this, I effectively reduced my hourly rate, which is what I normally tell you not to do. In this situation, it is all about filling up your books during down times, don't give these away and then book them during the height of your busy times. That is bad business. Put the full priced people in the busy times, and book these people during the slower times. You can even add the days or times available for this special coupon on the printout so you book your down times.

Let's face it, people love coupons. Even wealthy people like to feel like they are getting a deal. If what you are doing now isn't filling your books, then what does it hurt to try it? I consider this a marketing expense. While taking half of the service price this one time, you are generating new clients and making money during times you might have sit around not earning any money. I consider this a very important step into increasing your profit because that is exactly what you are doing by using these coupons—increasing profit you might not have earned by sitting around.

Additionally, you are only handing these out to a select group of customers—your best customers. Don't hand these out to cheap tippers, or other bad customers. Hand these out to only the best customers, it isn't a guarantee, but it is more likely that high quality customers hang around potentially other high-quality customers. One time, when I used this coupon method of marketing, I gave a few to a council woman in our area who came to see me, I gave her a couple and she gave them to her office staff as gifts. All these women who came from her office were highly professional, sweet, and generous tippers—it worked out better than I could have imagined and I obtained new clients without much effort, and made money during times I would have otherwise been sitting around with no clients.

This is a simple step because it is adding profit to your bottom line, and by giving these out to only your high-quality clients. It in returns higher quality clients in most cases.

Step 11: Online Coupons/Daily Deals

I cringed just a bit when I thought about adding this one. It wouldn't be fair if I ignored this piece of the cash cow, it is a huge piece of the industry. While I think this particular online coupon craze and daily deals are killing our industry, it is another way to keep your books filled and your pockets full of money during rough times. I don't recommend these online coupons unless you absolutely need the coupons to drastically increase revenue.

I'm not going to mention any names here, but I am sure you are acutely aware of these sites. A consumer buys an online coupon from their computer or phone, and in seconds they have a great deal for a fraction of the price. They have what seems like an infinite amount of time to use the coupon in the future, and the deals are great at the expense of the esthetician.

Quick Tip: Style Seat is now offering a similar service. They refer someone to you, and they retain 50%. However, all future bookings you keep at 100% of the earnings. The benefit of using Style Seat is that the shoppers aren't necessarily looking for rock bottom prices, so many of the referrals are full priced treatments as opposed to these online sites that you have to deeply discount to get them to purchase plus pay a 50% fee to the site.

What you may not know, as a business you only get 50% of the already reduced price. For example, if you offer a facial and brow wax reduced price of $40.00, you already reduced the price to a more than favorable amount, but the coupon giant also takes 50% of that leaving you with a whopping $20.00 plus tip. Now, these coupon sites do a great job reminding their customers to tip based on the true treatment costs (which they provide customers), but most customers tip based on what they actually paid.

Sounds like I don't like them, right? You would be correct. I don't like them. I have used them, and I was disappointed with them. However, with that said, I wanted to mention them in my steps because they can be effective in just generating some cash. This is a very personal choice, and there are schools of thought for and against it.

The people against it-- they believe it is destroying the quality of the industry. I agree. The estheticians offer such low prices, it makes it hard to compete and stay in business. In addition, many of the services are cheapened because let's face it, when an esthetician lowers their prices to bare bones, the quality surely comes down. The ugly side of these coupon sites, the one no one talks about is the lack of quality clients. Some of my worse clients have been from coupon sites; they are more fickle than the ones paying full price (I know hard to believe) and they think nothing of showing up late, and forget about them buying retail—nope they want everything at a fraction of the price.

What about loyalty? Very few of these clients are loyal, I had a few who were good about coming back but only at the same price that they first purchased the coupon for. Sure, at this point I was making more because there was no split with the coupon company, but it was way below market value, and that's a huge problem because once these people think of your services a bargain price, they don't want to pay the true price. They are coupon junkies, and they generally aren't loyal, it is all about the next best deal.

Why would I list this as a step if I dislike the coupon giants? Well, as much as it makes me cringe, you can still add extra money by doing this. **It is extra cash in your pocket during slow times**. If you are just starting out on your own, it might get you through the days when there isn't a client in sight. Some money is better than no money, and while I offer these online coupon sites with caution, I want you to be aware that they do work in terms of keeping your books filled and money in your pocket. Albeit, it isn't as much money as you could make filling your books at full price, it generates income that you might otherwise not make if your books aren't full.

When I did this, I made sure to ALWAYS offer at the time of booking an upgrade…this is where the REAL MONEY can be made with these online coupon sites. Let's say someone bought a facial and brow wax combo, when they called me to book, I would tell them that this month I am offering an aromatherapy add on for $20.00, or I am offering a 30-minute back facial for a great price of $35.00, but it is only available for a short time and as an add-on. I came up with many different ideas, but the back facial seems to be one that people added on the most. Sometimes I would add a peel on for $20.00 with any facial as well, and that one seemed popular too.

Now, let's say I sold a coupon for $40.00 and I only get $20.00, but now I sold a $35.00 back facial (this is assuming your work for yourself—if you are employed you can bring these ideas to your boss) I now am making $55.00 for an 1.5 of work as opposed to only $20.00. Even better was when I made that $20.00 plus another $20.00 in that same hour, then I just double the money in that one hour. That helps out a lot! As far as tipping, some will tip more as they should for the additional services, but with some of these coupon junkies, you don't see a lot added to your tip amount because they still tip only on what they originally purchased.

If you decide to use online coupon sites, make it work for you. Don't be afraid to ask them when they are booking to do an add-on. I had some people tell me "no" and then when they arrived they would ask me if I still had time for that add-on. **About 50% of these clients will say "yes" and then you've taken a cruddy coupon and turned it into more money in your pocket.** Sure, it might not be as much as booking without the coupon, but it is still generating more money than just using the coupon only.

Don't forget retail as well. I don't care how cheap these coupon people are, I still always tried to sell them retail…in fact, these people need it more than your upscale clients because they tend to buy over-the-counter junk more. Most of my coupon people turned me down for the retail, but some said "yes" and it was more money in my pocket.

Quick Tip: Remind all clients that they can purchase the same coupon directly through you in the future. You cut out the middle man of the coupon site, but you also get a 100% of the coupon price instead of paying 50% to the coupon site.

I don't like these coupon sites, and I would strive to eliminate them from your practice as soon as you are generating enough income, but in the meantime, use them to generate money and fill those books. Please don't be shy about asking about those upgrades—those upgrades are the bread and butter of these coupons. If you just take these coupons, and you don't try to push the limit and offer other services/upgrades you are giving money away. It is an impulsive purchase, you have them on the phone to book, or you have them in your treatment room on the table, don't be pushy but always ask them. If they said "no" at the time of booking, gently remind them of the great deal you are offering when they arrive, sometimes they make that impulse purchase. Remember, they are already impulse purchasers who purchase coupons on their phone, so it is likely they will impulse by again if they think it is a great deal.

This is the top way to make these coupons work for you—generate more income by turning the ugly side of these coupons into the beautiful side of making more money. We've established that I don't like these coupons, but I think they definitely deserve to be listed as a step here. For a lot of estheticians, these coupons help keep them afloat, and for many it generates a whole new piece of the financial pie.

I wouldn't make these coupons your sole source of attracting new clients—I think the goal should be to attract high quality and loyal clients. I would recommend picking your slow days to offer time slots to these clients, and save your best days for the full-priced client. You want to make the full-priced client happier because they are more likely to return, the coupon junkie client just wants to redeem the service paid for. It's a step I recommend only for slow times.

Step 12: Facebook Power

Who doesn't love Facebook? People can't live without Facebook, it is like the morning coffee—there would be a lot of cranky people if we shut down Facebook for just one day! Facebook is powerful. I think most of us are getting our news from Facebook more than any other source these days.

I love Facebook. It is fun scrolling down through it, and I love seeing the ads that pop up. I used it in my own treatment room, and I created a business Facebook page. I also paid to "boost" my ads and blogs. I would run my specials through Facebook, and I used specific categories to draw people in.

Facebook is either loved or hated by estheticians who run their own business. Some feel like all they get are likes for the money spent, while others feel like they actually get clients. The costs are low, and you can run a seven-day ad for as little as $7.00. It is very affordable advertising.

For me personally, I used them and I ran ads every month. It generated new leads for me, and I booked many clients from Facebook with spending little money. I think that had I invested even more money in Facebook ads, I would have seen even greater results. So for me, I had a great experience with them in terms of generating a new income stream of clients that I couldn't find on my own.

Another thing that is great about Facebook is that you can run contests on your business page, and you can generate new bookings/increased revenue by holding a contest (check your state laws about contests). It is a great way to get people interested in in your business, and getting the buzz around it.

Step 13: Networking Groups Work

This step, getting involved in networking groups is one that surprised me the most. I never wanted to venture out into the networking world. It feels a little fake as people come together for the sole purpose of selling each other. Estheticians can join business networking groups just like any other business professional.

What surprised me the most was to find women in these groups who were so called "skin care experts" because they sold multi-level marketing skin care and make-up products. It never crossed my mind that MLM reps were allowed into networking groups.

These women were purporting themselves as facial experts, and people in the group (mostly women) were actually buying the skin care and make-up products. I actually had a rep tell me she does exactly what an esthetician does, with the exception of holding a license. It made me want to be a part of these groups even more, I wanted to get the right information out there about skin care, and I wanted to sell professional grade products.

I decided to try a few out. I initially tried a "Speed Networking Group" and a business networking group where you had to be invited by someone else. With these groups, you have to pay some type of fee, it is usually a write off on taxes (check with your tax adviser). With the speed networking, I had to pay a one-time fee to go to the event. It was a place where you have so many seconds to give your speech about what you do. Is it appropriate? I wondered this myself, why would business owners want anything to do with esthetic services? Well, surprisingly you will find many businesses that are complementary to your own business, for instance, I met massage therapists, aroma therapists, acupuncturists, etc. at these events. I also met Realtors, this is a great group of people to get involved in with esthetics. When we spoke about those free coupons with the upgrades earlier, this is a great group of people to give some coupons to. Why? They give them to their best clients, these are people who are new to the area and probably don't know any estheticians, what a great way to get some referrals. Also, don't forget the men in the group, they have wives, sisters, and mothers that could use that coupon.

In some of these groups, you will find that you will need to give a speech about what you do, or provide some type of information session on a topic about skin care. It sounds hard at first, but the topics are endless. I found that doing an anti-aging topic usually fits the bill for most women in these networking groups, and ending your speech with free samples is a great way to get their attention.

How do these groups increase your profit? These groups are designed around building your business networks, and they are designed on referral basis—they generally refer from within. The benefit is that you will almost always be the only esthetician in these groups, some groups have a strict rule that there can only be one of each profession. What about the MLM people? Aren't they considered skin care experts? Usually they go under a different category, and they are of no consequence to an esthetician because they don't truly understand how the skin and products work together.

The money that comes from networking groups usually isn't instantaneous, rather it takes time to reap the rewards. As you build your group of contacts, you increase your potential for clients and referrals, and that's how you increase your profits. You are generating a whole new piece of the market that you might not have had before, these are people that will come to you themselves, or invite family, friends, and colleagues to do so. This is an opportunity to give out coupons, and when you give out the free coupons, we know from my own experience that most people upgrade and pay the difference for an hour long facial. It is also an opportunity to demonstrate your products, and you can bring products to sell at these events. Remember, most people are impulse buyers, and if you have the product available for them to see and touch, they are more likely to purchase.

While networking isn't a super-fast method to increasing your profits, it certainly plays an important role in growing your profit tree. If you are sitting around your treatment room, doing nothing but taking care of the current clients, you are never expanding your potential financial gain. You are giving away money to someone else. At first, these groups seem intimidating, but I promise you that people will regard you as the expert, and these busy people will want to investigate what you have to offer—what you bring to the group that is unique.

Here are some business networking groups that may be of interest to you. Remember, most cost money to join as a member, or they cost per session fees, it is up to you to speak to your tax adviser to see if you can write them off as marketing costs.

(1) Local Chamber of Commerce (one of my favorites)
(2) BNI (one of my favorites)
(3) Meet Up
(4) Christian Business Networking
(5) International Executive Association
(6) Rotary Club
(7) National Association of Women Business Owners
(8) MOMS Club (while not a business club, it is a great club to recruit moms)
(9) MOPS (another great club to recruit ladies for treatments)
(10) Civic, church, and volunteer clubs/activities.

Quick Tip: Getting involved in networking groups, civic clubs, church clubs, or even moms' groups is the ability to branch out and have that many more potential clients. It helps expand your database of perspective clients, and as you turn the prospects into clients, the power of the networking groups is in the money that you earn. In my experience, the fees to join these groups are minimal in comparison to the earnings possible.

Networking groups are so much more than just money, it is a great place for people to gather and build friendships outside of the business. In many cases, a lot of estheticians work a very lonely career, the client sleeps much of the time, and the esthetician is busy in between cleaning up between clients that it is hard to build sustainable relationships at the place of employment. The networking group allows for another source of a revenue stream as well as building new friendships.

Step 14: Become a Skin Care Distributor

Of all the tips, this is one that I learned after giving money away! As professionals, we can open wholesale accounts and generally get 50% off retail prices. That's fantastic, in fact, when we retail products we literally get to double the price of products. If you don't own the spa then you will likely get a retail commission split, which we covered in step 5, either way that step is extremely important, but this step is different. I am not talking about selling a product in just the spa, I am talking about becoming a part-time rep for a skin care line while working in the treatment room. Why would you want to do both? It means more money in your pocket. When you become a distributor of a skin care line, and you sell that line in your place of business you get freebies and extra discounts that non-distributors don't get. In other words, that same product you are purchasing for your back bar and your retail becomes less expensive, in turn that brings you in more money. I never knew this. I just happily went along with either using what was given to me at the spa, or when I worked for myself I gladly handed over my money to buy product from another rep. That was a huge mistake, I just turned money away!

I turned money away because I didn't realize that when you become a distributor not only do you usually get deeper discounts, you get free samples (hint: share with clients), and you are in control of the pricing of the retail products. You don't have to follow any rules from the distributor you are buying from —you only have to follow the rules set by the company, if they have specific rules. I am talking about the way you package and charge for the retail products—get creative and package them in a way that makes them a cash cow—gift baskets, baggies with retail products and a facial brush, or anything you can think of to make that product line more valuable to customers.

Quick Tip: No sales experience? That's okay. There are plenty of start-up companies looking to work on a split commission plan with

estheticians…this helps you make extra cash, save in your treatment and retail areas, and it helps you gain experience if you ever want to work for a bigger skin care company. Check local ads, Facebook, and other social media outlets to see if there are any start-up companies looking to bring on estheticians for their team.

I decided to stop buying skin care products at regular wholesale after I started working part-time for a distributor. I wanted to offer the product line that I felt like I represented, and I wanted to increase my profit. I bought wholesale at 50% off with normal professional brands, but as a distributor I got 75% off retail. With that said, I would keep a couple products on hand for the people that might not benefit from that particular product line that I sold, not every product line is for everyone, and I won't push something that I don't believe is right for that person.

The second reason that I made the switch, money, let's face it the discounts and freebies were worth a lot more than buying wholesale from another vendor. It was a smart move for me. Not only did I lower my costs substantially in the treatment room, I increased my retail sales. Not only was I better educated about the product line because I had an insider's training on the products, but I also knew how to retail it better and how to price it based on my training with the company. My retail sales increased dramatically and the money I earned exponentially increased at the same time because I was rockin the retail and cutting costs in the treatment room.

I wish I had known about this little secret years prior, but lesson learned. What about people who don't want to be a sales rep? What about creating your own line? There are so many skin care manufacturing companies out there today, and instead of creating a line it is more like branding your line. You pick the products and then pick the labels, and then you brand that line in your establishment.

How does creating your own label help you? It cuts out the middle man, the distributor that you are buying from and your costs are generally lower. Secondly, it brands you—your spa is now associated with a skin care brand, and you can decide on the prices of those products vs. a distributor who will tell you a retail price for the product. It allows you a little more control, and quite frankly it seems like a lot of fun. I don't know because I have yet to venture off into that realm of this industry yet, but if you have a creative spirit, it might be a good place to start to increase your profits.

If people believe in you, then they will most likely believe in your brand and keep coming back for your brand instead buying Robin McGraw on HSN or Aveeno at the local drugstore because Jennifer Aniston represents it in commercials.

In this industry, we are competing with so many celebrity skin care lines, we all know those lines aren't the same caliber as our professional grade lines, but they sell because of branding. Who doesn't want skin like Jennifer Aniston or Robin McGraw?

Do your customers love your skin? Do they love you? Do you have a rapport with them? If you do they will most likely buy your product line, which means more money for you, but more importantly it means keeping your clients on a skin care line that you believe in and know it works for their skin type.

This piece of the cash cow is flooded with so many over-the-counter and professional lines that sometimes it seems like there is no market place for anything more, but if you are determined to increase your profits, and you believe in your product line (whether you sell as a distributor or create your own line) then why shouldn't you get a piece of the cash cow too? Remember, you are an expert and people want your knowledge and what you have to offer, give it to them and increase your revenue stream.

Final Thoughts

I am no different than any of you out there; the only difference is I put my experiences on paper. I want you to be a rock star esthetician, and I want you to be able to command top dollar from employers. We estheticians need to band together and support each other.

I wish you much success, and the gift of loving what you do. There is no better feeling in the world than waking up each day, going to work and it not being able to work at all. This career has the potential to be that gift to you, and while loving what you do doesn't pay the bills, it is the business savviness that will secure your future doing what you love. Open the financial flood gates and prepare for a bright financial future.

Best Wishes